help**me**
UNDERSTAND ™

Hiding *Emotions* &
Learning *Authenticity*™

REAL
mvpkids ®

Leo's Pent-Up Feelings

SOPHIA DAY®

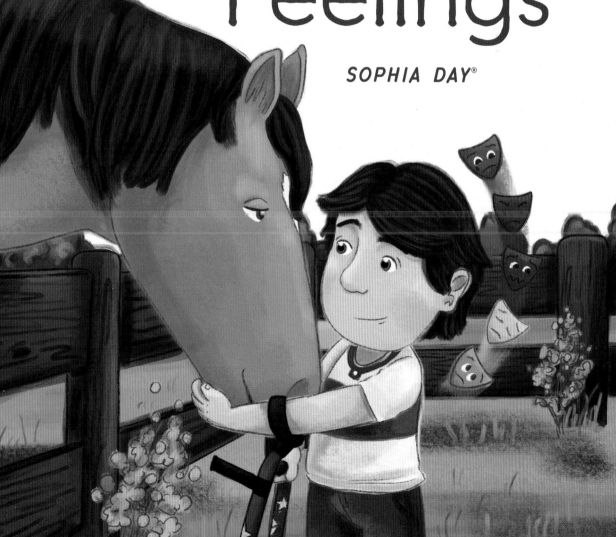

Written by Megan Johnson *Illustrated by* Stephanie Strouse

WELCOME to the WORLD OF

mvpkids®

Entertainment with PURPOSE™

Everything we create is with the intention of nurturing a child's character. Our mission is to equip parents, teachers and caregivers to engage with kids through inspiring entertainment.

| nurture LITERACY™ | cultivate MENTORSHIP™ | inspire CHARACTER® | expand EDUCATION™ | enrich ENTERTAINMEN |

help**me**
UNDERSTAND™

Hiding *Emotions* &
Learning *Authenticity*™

REAL

mvpkids®

Leo's Pent-Up Feelings

SOPHIA DAY®

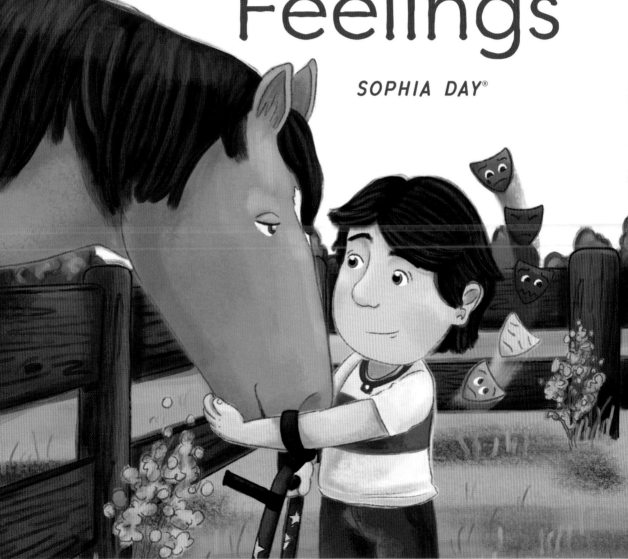

Written by Megan Johnson *Illustrated by* Stephanie Strouse

The Sophia Day® Creative Team-
Megan Johnson, Stephanie Strouse,
Kayla Pearson, Timothy Zowada, Mel Sauder

A **special thank you** to our team of reviewers who graciously
give us feedback, edits and help ensure that our products
remain accurate, applicable and genuinely diverse.

Published and Distributed by MVP Kids Media, LLC -
Mesa, Arizona, USA
Printed by Prosperous Printing Inc. -
Shenzhen, China

Designed by Stephanie Strouse

DOM July 2019, Job # 02-009-01

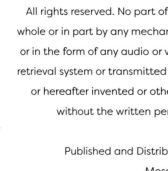

May your childhood be filled with adventure, your days with hope and your learnings with wisdom, and may you continuously grow as an MVP Kid, preparing to lead a responsible, meaningful life.

–SOPHIA DAY

Leo could smell Esperanza Stables before he could see it. Not in a bad way, just in a **_not-in-the-city-anymore_** sort of way.

Usually, Leo felt a freedom on horseback
that he didn't feel anywhere else.
With reins in his hands instead of crutches,
he was just the same as anyone else.

But today,
Leo didn't feel the same kind of freedom.
Some big things had changed in his life recently,
and Leo didn't know how to handle his feelings.

He spent most of his time feeling lost and hopeless.
Sometimes he didn't even know what he was
feeling. He kept everything **pent up inside** and
covered it with a smile.

"Hi, Abuela." Leo greeted Mrs. González cheerfully, but he felt like a liar.

"Welcome! Gabby is riding with us today," she said. "Why don't you go finish the grooming with her?"

Gabby lived at the farm
where her grandma
ran Esperanza Stables.
She was a good friend,
but Leo didn't
feel much like
chatting today.

There was too much on his mind for him to think clearly, much less talk to anyone. If he started talking, all his feelings might just spill out.

"Hi, Leo," Gabby said cheerfullly.

"Hey," Leo said, avoiding her gaze.

Apple stamped a hoof and startled Leo.

"What's gotten into her today?" he asked Gabby.

"I don't know. She's been fine all morning, but she seems unsettled now."

Apple continued stamping her hoof and shaking her mane.

Gabby realized that Leo wasn't
his usual self today, either.
"You know, a horse responds to the rider's feelings.
Are you doing okay?"

"Come on, let's get to riding." Leo avoided the question,
determined not to talk about his feelings.

They saddled Apple, and Leo prepared to mount.

Apple made a small protest when
Leo shifted into the saddle.

"How are you, Leo?" Abuela asked.

"Just fine. I'm always happy to be here."
Leo tightened his grip on the reins, trying to
control his carefully balanced smile.

"It's okay to not always be happy," Abuela said.

"I said I'm fine," he snapped.

If one more person asks me how I'm doing, **I'll fall apart,** *Leo thought.*

"Look! No hands!" Gabby dropped the reins and rode figure eights in the arena with her arms out.

"How does the horse know where to go when she does that?" Leo asked, holding the reins even more firmly.

"Horses are intuitive*.
They are very good at understanding
their rider, if your mind is clear,"
Abuela said.

***Intuitive** - able to use clues to understand something without needing to be told.

Leo's mind was anything but clear.

Nothing in his life had felt clear since — Leo didn't want to think about it. Right now, everything was blurry as he blinked back tears.

Well, I won't be letting go of these reins anytime soon, he thought.

He must have accidentally kicked as he reined in his feelings. The next thing he knew, Apple had startled and *bolted* for the exit gate.

Leo pulled back on the reins to stop, but she jumped right over the fence and headed off to the trails.

Leo was **scared**. He had never felt
so out of control. His **fear** was too big
to hide, and he began to yell.

"Stop, Apple! Stop!"

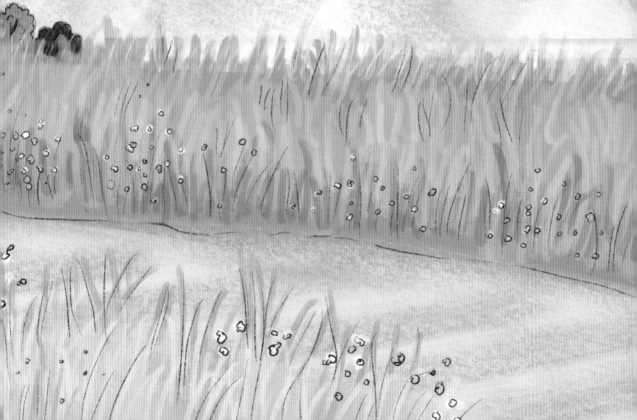

Apple slowed to a stop and Leo draped his arms around her neck. He could feel that she was scared, too. "It's okay, girl. We're okay. That was scary, but we're safe."

Saying it out loud changed something.
No longer pent up, all of his feelings began to spill
out with tears. "You know what else is scary, girl?
Everything has changed, and I'm **scared**
I'll never feel happy again."

He felt safe talking to Apple. "I'm **sad** that life is different now, since — " It was difficult to talk about, even to a horse. "And I'm **angry**, too. Why did everything have to happen to me? It's not fair!"

Leo talked through every one of his feelings. It amazed him that all at once he could feel **scared**, **sad**, **angry**, lonely and confused.

For a moment, Leo felt guilty. He didn't want
to burden others with his feelings. But Apple
didn't seem burdened at all. You see, whether
it's a horse or a person who loves you, it's more difficult
for them to guess about your feelings than to listen.

Sharing feelings
is a gift,
not a burden.

Giving names to his feelings helped Leo sort things out. He felt like he could see clearly for the first time in a long time. He **knew** that he would have to continue to talk about his feelings so he wouldn't be lost in them.

Gripping the reins, he looked around for the path that led to the stables. He wasn't at all sure where they were or which way led back. Leo was lost, but he wasn't hopeless.

Leo sighed and dropped the reins on Apple's neck.

"Go home," he said.

Abuela and Gabby, who had been watching from the trail, met him on the way back. **"Look at you! No reins!"** Gabby said.

"No hands!" he replied, as
he stretched his arms out to give
her a high-five.

"Are you okay?" Abuela asked.
"Yes and no. I'm not hurt.
I'm also not okay. Can we talk?"

He had trusted Apple to guide him when he was lost. Now he realized he could trust the people who love him when he feels lost, too. Abuela guided him through talking about his feelings. "When Apple jumped the fence, I felt scared because I thought you might get hurt," she said.

"When I talked with Apple, I felt safe because she wouldn't judge my feelings."

"Your feelings are safe with us, too!" Gabby said.

Leo confided* in them about why he was feeling **scared**, **sad**, **angry**, lonely and confused. He was relieved he didn't have to keep it all pent up anymore. Apple's escape had freed them both!

***Confide** - to tell something secret or personal to someone you trust.

You're putting on a smile,
A mask to face the world,
Hoping all the while
Your happy act will hold.

Avoiding those who love you,
Pretending you're okay
Those feelings all pent up inside
Will let loose when it breaks.

Every feeling has a purpose,
And when you try to hide,
You just increase your burdens
As you hold it all inside.

It's a gift to share your feelings,
Trusting others with your pain.
You'll be on the trail to healing
As you let up on the reins.

If you're not sure how to do it
You can try to say,
"**When** this happens, **I feel** that
Because it seems this way."

When you're lost and life feels blurry,
Don't try to hide away.
Trust your guides. Don't worry.
They will help you find your way.

LEARN & DISCUSS

Big changes, tragedies and losses are full of hard emotions, and talking about them is important. Leo learned to release his pent-up feelings, and you can, too!

> Some big things have happened in my life recently, and I was working really hard to keep my feelings pent up. I wanted to act like everything was okay, even though I had some big feelings.

Have big changes happened in your life? How did it make you feel?

Why do people sometimes choose to hide their feelings?

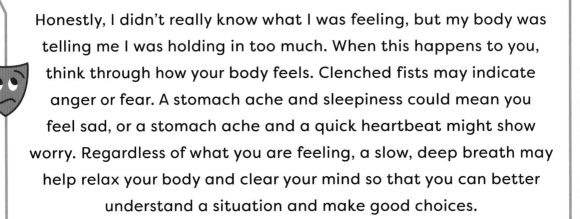

> Honestly, I didn't really know what I was feeling, but my body was telling me I was holding in too much. When this happens to you, think through how your body feels. Clenched fists may indicate anger or fear. A stomach ache and sleepiness could mean you feel sad, or a stomach ache and a quick heartbeat might show worry. Regardless of what you are feeling, a slow, deep breath may help relax your body and clear your mind so that you can better understand a situation and make good choices.

Act out different emotions and think about or describe to someone how your body feels when you act happy, angry, sad or scared. Describe what happens to the muscles in your face.

How does your stomach feel? Are your hands in fists or relaxed?

What else do you notice?

Did you know that sharing your feelings with others is an important part of staying healthy? Studies show that people who keep their feelings pent up become sick more often, and it can have a long-term impact on their health.

Whom can you talk with when you need someone to listen?

What are some characteristics of a safe person and a good listener?

One of the reasons I kept my feelings to myself was because I didn't want to burden other people. I was afraid that if I shared the difficult things in my life with someone else, it would somehow make them upset, too. Then I realized that when people care, they want to know how I feel. Sharing feelings is a gift, not a burden.

How do you feel when friends trust you enough to tell you how they feel about changes or challenges in their lives?

People aren't always as good as horses about understanding how you feel. You may have to explain. I like to use this form to help me express my feelings. When _____ , I feel _____ because _____ . For example, "When I ride Apple without reins, I feel confident, because I can trust her to navigate."

Now it's your turn to try. Think of some sentences you can use to express your feelings to someone you trust. You could also try writing in a journal. When _____, I feel _____ because _____ .

How can you help your child release pent-up feelings?

Recognize if your child is struggling. There can be many indicators that a child needs help releasing their feelings. Pay attention to these possible indicators:

- A change in appetite, either loss or increase, may indicate the presence of additional stress. Similarly, a dramatic increase or decrease in weight that is unexpected for their developmental stage may indicate a presence of higher adrenaline or cortisol levels.

- Frequent tantrums are a good sign that your child has unexpressed feelings. Look beyond the tantrum and try to discern what may be going on in the background. A child may express anger when trying to cover up other feelings of anxiety, rejection or sadness.

- Lack of focus or distractibility may indicate that your child is avoiding the opportunity to truly experience his or her feelings. Take notice if increased distractibility occurs after experiencing loss or change. Over-commitment to activities or constant rushing around is a coping mechanism to avoid one's feelings.

Evaluate your own feeling biases. No feeling is inherently bad, and every feeling has a purpose. If you have made a practice of avoiding feelings, it's likely your child has picked up on this attitude. Make sure you are sending a message that it is okay to talk about all feelings.

Start small. Expressing feelings does not always come naturally. Start by modeling small acknowledgements of feelings. Simple expressions like, "I woke up feeling rested today. How did you sleep?" or "I'm excited about dinner tonight. It's my favorite meal." Show that feelings are an appropriate topic of conversation in your family. Ask your child to share a small feeling like this with you every day. Resist the urge to correct a feeling if your child says something like, "I'm angry because I don't like dinner." As sharing becomes a habit and children see that feelings can be safe, they are more likely to come to you with bigger feelings, too.

Provide structure for those who struggle with expressing an emotional thought. Try the formula "When _____, I feel _____ because _____." For example, "When you don't eat what I prepared for dinner, I feel disrespected because I worked hard to give you this meal." Or "When we play games as a family, I feel happy because I enjoy spending time with you."

Shared activities are a less threatening environment than sitting down formally to talk about feelings. If you want to get your child talking, play a game, go for a drive or take a hike. The activity will take some of the focus off of the conversation, allowing for a more relaxed atmosphere.

Seek help if your child's avoidance of feelings is concerning you. Children benefit from having safe adults they can talk to in addition to their parents. Consider asking a trusted friend, teacher or family member to help mentor your child. Follow your instinct if you feel like your child needs a professional therapy evaluation.

Meet the

mvpkids®

featured in

Leo's Pent-Up Feelings™

LEO RUSSO

GABBY GONZÁLEZ

Also featuring...

CLAUDIA RUSSO
"Mom"

ROSA MARIA GONZÁLEZ
"Abuela"

APPLE

HELADO

Grow up with our **mvp**kids

Our **CELEBRATE**™ board books for toddlers and preschoolers focus on social, emotional, educational and physical needs. Helpful Teaching Tips are included in each book to equip parents to guide their children deeper into the subject of each book.

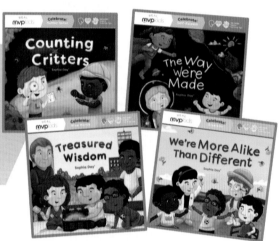

Our **Celebrate!**™ paperback books for Pre-K to Grade 2 focus on social and emotional needs. Helpful Teaching Tips are included in each book to equip parents, teachers and counselors. Also available are expertly written curriculum and interactive e-book apps.

Our **Help Me Become**™ series for early elementary readers tells three short stories in each book of our MVP Kids® inspiring character growth. Each story concludes with a discussion guide to help the child process the story and apply the concepts.

Help your children grow in understanding emotions by collecting the entire **Help Me Understand™** series!

*Our **Help Me Understand™** series for elementary readers shares the stories of our MVP Kids® learning to understand and manage specific emotions. Readers will gain tools to take responsibility for their own emotions and develop healthy relationships.*

Lucas Tames the Anger Dragon

Miriam Lassoes the Worry Whirlwind

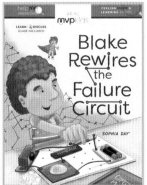

Blake Rewires the Failure Circuit

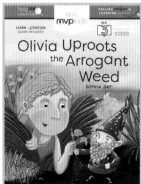

Olivia Uproots the Arrogant Weed

Yong Breaks Out of the Boredom Box

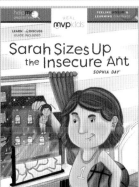

Sarah Sizes Up the Insecure Ant

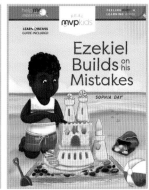

Ezekiel Builds on his Mistakes

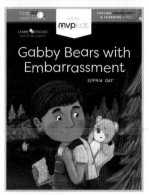

Gabby Bears with Embarrassment

Leo's Pent-Up Feelings

Annie's Jar of Patience

Liam Conquers Fort Grudge

*Learn about our **Social and Emotional Learning Curriculum**, puppets and more at **www.mvpkidsED.com**.*

*To view our full list of products, visit **www.mvpkids.com**.*

LEO RUSSO

FRANKIE RUSSO

YONG CHEN

JULIA ROJAS

GABBY GONZÁLEZ

AANYA PATEL

ANNIE JAMES

BLAKE JAMES

SARAH COHEN-GOLDSTEIN

LUCAS MILLER

LEBRON MILLER

FAITH JORDAN

MIRIAM NASSER

EZEKIEL JORDAN

OLIVIA WAGNER

LIAM JOHNSON

Get to know our MVP Kids®!
You will learn and grow with them from book to book. Each MVP Kid® has a personal back story and a unique personality, making it easier for kids of all kinds to see themselves and their friends within our books!

www.mvpkids.com

Real MVP Kids

@realMVPkids